Hope Recovery

The Twelve Keys of Faith-Based Recovery

How to Be Successful in Recovery By Embracing Key Biblical Truths

Booklet Edition

Greg Schmalhofer

Dedication

The Twelve Keys of Faith-Based Recovery is dedicated to the late Pastor Walt Heidecker, the founding pastor of the faith-based Discovery Recovery group.

Table of Contents

Acknowledgements

The twelve keys of faith-based recovery were first listed as a chart in the 100 day devotional book *The Hope Recovery Devotional: There is Always Hope with God* (Greg Schmalhofer, 2021). This book, *The Twelve Keys of Faith-Based Recovery*, presents twelve new lessons combined into an easy-to-read book for a new focused look at these twelve key lessons of faith-based recovery.[1]

The Twelve Keys of Faith-Based Recovery is planned to be available in multiple editions.

Pocket Edition   (4.25 x 7.00)
Booklet Edition   (5.00 x 8.00)
Large Print Edition   (6.00 x 9.00)
Kindle/Ebook

Also, I would like to express many thanks to all of our dear friends of the Discovery Recovery group for their overwhelming kindness, support, and encouragement for these two books of faith-based recovery.

Hope Recovery

The Twelve Keys Of Faith-Based Recovery

Introduction

Welcome to *The Twelve Keys of Faith-Based Recovery*. I am so glad you are taking the time to read this book as it presents what I have found are the twelve key biblical truths that are so important to help people be successful in recovery. These twelve key biblical truths share the faith-based messages that are so critical for those in recovery. This book will guide you through the biblical principles that build one upon the other that ultimately lead you to the loving God of the Bible, the true "Higher Power", success in recovery, and a brand new life with God. These twelve keys of faith-based recovery integrate recovery principles and basic Bible truths so that you can put your hope and trust in God to grow in your recovery and in your faith as well.

The Twelve Steps, as presented in the books of *Alcoholics Anonymous* and *Narcotics Anonymous,* are each referenced throughout this book as they both speak of God and having a spiritual experience with God. The books of AA and NA are both outstanding books that guide you through the Twelve Steps. This book, *The Twelve Keys of Faith-Based Recovery,* helps you take this spiritual experience with God even further. Each of the twelve faith-based lessons includes a Scripture reading, recovery principle, recovery quotes, biblical message, additional Bible passages, and closing thoughts to summarize each lesson. As you read through these twelve keys of faith-based recovery, consider each lesson and message for you personally and remember that the God of the Bible is a loving, caring, and compassionate God and he wants to help you be successful in recovery and to have a brand new life through faith in Christ.

Regardless of where you are at with God today, I encourage you to embrace each of *The Twelve Keys of Faith-Based Recovery* and to be open to the possibility of bringing God into your life. With God in your life, you can indeed be successful in recovery. Commit today to leave your past in the past and to do everything necessary to be successful in recovery and to have a brand new life in Christ.

<u>The Twelve Keys of Faith-Based Recovery (1-4)</u>

1) There is a God in heaven.

- *Psalm 46:10 "Be still, and know that I am God."*
- There is a God in heaven; and he is a loving, caring, and compassionate God who wants to help you.

2) There is always hope with God.

- *Isaiah 41:10 "Fear not, for I am with you; Be not dismayed, for I am your God. I will strengthen you, Yes, I will help you." (NKJV)*
- With God there is always hope. You are not alone, God is with you and he wants to help you.

3) Do you want to get well?

- *John 5:6 "When Jesus saw him lying there and learned that he had been in this condition for a long time, he asked him, 'Do you want to get well?'"*
- Do you want to get well and are you willing to do whatever is necessary to be successful in recovery?

4) Recovery is possible with God.

- *Philippians 4:13 "I can do all things through Christ who strengthens me." (NKJV)*
- Don't let you past dictate your future. With God recovery is absolutely possible.

5) God wants to forgive you.

- *<u>Psalm 103:10-12</u> "He does not deal with us according to our sins.... [11] For as high as the heavens are above the earth, so great is his steadfast love toward those who fear him; [12] as far as the east is from the west, so far does he remove our transgressions from us.(ESV)*
- Regardless of what you have done in the past, God wants to forgive you!

6) Seek God and you will find him.

- *<u>Jeremiah 29:13</u> "You will seek me and find me when you seek me with all your heart."*
- Seek God with all of your heart and you will find him.

7) Jesus is the true Higher Power.

- *<u>John 14:6</u> "Jesus answered, "I am the way and the truth and the life. No one comes to the Father except through me."*
- Jesus is the way, the truth, and the life and Jesus is the true Higher Power.

8) Make a decision to put your faith in Jesus.

- *<u>John 3:16</u> "For God so loved the world that he gave his one and only Son, that whoever believes in him shall not perish but have eternal life."*
- Put your faith and trust in Jesus as the true Higher Power.

9) Surround yourself with like-minded people.

- *1 Corinthians 15:33 "Do not be misled: "Bad company corrupts good character."*
- Surround yourself with like-minded people that share your desire to be clean and sober and share your love for God.

10) God made you for a purpose.

- *Jeremiah 29:11 "'For I know the plans I have for you,' declares the Lord, 'plans to prosper you and not to harm you, plans to give you hope and a future.'"*
- God has made you for a purpose; consider what has God called you to do?

11) Peace that surpasses all understanding.

- *Philippians 4:7 "And the peace of God, which surpasses all understanding, will guard your hearts and your minds in Christ Jesus." (ESV)*
- You will still have struggles, but with God in your life you can have 'a peace that surpasses all understanding'.

12) Continue to trust God no matter what.

- *Proverbs 3:5-6 "Trust in the Lord with all your heart; do not depend on your own understanding. ^{6} Seek his will in all you do, and he will show you which path to take."(NLT)*
- No matter what happens continue to put your faith and trust in God and he will give you guidance and wisdom.

There Is a God in Heaven

Be still, and know that I am God.
(Psalm 46:10 ESV)

===

"There is a God in heaven; and he is a
loving, caring, and compassionate God
who wants to help you."[2]
(The Hope Recovery Devotional)

===

"All I can say is that it's a Power greater than
myself. If pressed, all I can do is follow the
psalmist who said it long before me:
'Be still, and know that I am God.'"[3]
(Alcoholics Anonymous)

===

This first key of faith-based recovery is critical, but honestly, they are all critical just in different ways. The first key of faith-based recovery is to accept and acknowledge that there is a God in heaven. This does not mean that you have God all figured out or that you now know all about God, but you simply acknowledge that yes, there is a God in heaven. This is a basic truth of the Bible and it is also the truth of the widespread evidence of the created world all around you. The truth of the Bible is wonderfully matched with the abundant evidence of a divinely created world. All of this is evidence of an amazing and all powerful God.

This is indeed a great and comforting truth. However, the message of the Bible goes even further not only is there a God in heaven, but he is a loving, caring, and compassionate God and he does indeed want to help you. I ask you to consider not only is there a God in heaven, but he does indeed want to help you. Regardless of where you are in your recovery, I encourage you to simply follow the words of Psalm 46:10 to "Be still, and know that I am God." You can have confidence that there is a God and that he wants to help you. This passage tells you to be still and to have confidence there is a God. You can rest in him; you can trust him, because he is indeed a loving, caring, and compassionate God who wants to help you be successful in recovery and over any struggle of life. Indeed, it all starts with acknowledging that there is a God in heaven and that he wants to help you!

Additional Bible Passages
Key #1 - There Is a God in Heaven

Genesis 1:1
In the beginning, God created the heavens and the earth.

Romans 1:20
For since the creation of the world God's invisible qualities—his eternal power and divine nature—have been clearly seen, being understood from what has been made, so that people are without excuse.

Psalm 19:1
The heavens declare the glory of God; the skies proclaim the work of his hands.

Isaiah 41:13
For I am the Lord your God who takes hold of your right hand and says to you, Do not fear; I will help you.

Psalm 86:15
But you, Lord, are a compassionate and gracious God, slow to anger, abounding in love and faithfulness.

Closing Thoughts
Key #1 - There Is a God in Heaven

1) Embrace the simple truth that there is a God in heaven. The created world all around you is evidence of a divine and all powerful God.

2) Not only is there a God, but he is a loving, caring, and compassionate God and he wants to help you.

3) You are not alone! God is with you and wants to help you in your recovery and in any struggle of life.

4) I encourage you to pause right now and to be still before God. Pray to God as never before. Perhaps, even with a simple prayer like "Please dear God help me!"

5) *Alcoholics Anonymous* speaks to this truth about God and states:
"Actually we were fooling ourselves, for deep down in every man, woman, and child, is the fundamental idea of God. It may be obscured by calamity, by pomp, by worship of other things, but in some form or other it is there. For faith in a Power greater than ourselves, and miraculous demonstrations of that power in human lives, are facts as old as man himself. We finally saw that faith in some kind of God was a part of our make-up, just as much as the feeling we have for a friend. Sometimes we had to search fearlessly, but He was there."[4]

There Is Always Hope with God

**Fear not, for I am with you;
Be not dismayed, for I am your God.
I will strengthen you, Yes, I will help you.
(Isaiah 41:10 NKJV)**

===

"With God there is always hope.
You are not alone, God is with you
and he wants to help you."[5]
(*The Hope Recovery Devotional*)

===

"My physical being has certainly
undergone a transformation, but the major
transformation has been spiritual.
The hopelessness has been replaced by a
bundant hope and sincere faith."[6]
(*Alcoholics Anonymous*)

===

By accepting there is a God in heaven, it is then possible to truly have hope. It is through this beginning step of faith that you can begin to understand the ultimate basis of hope. Your new found hope is not in just a wish or hope for good luck, but your hope is in the loving and all powerful God of the Bible.

The passage today explains further just where your true hope resides. This passage instructs you to be courageous and to "Fear not" because "I am with you". Do not be "dismayed, for I am your God." These words are intended to calm your fears and for you to put your hope and trust in God and not in your own power. In your own power you will always be lacking, but this passage of Isaiah 41:10 exclaims that God "will strengthen you" and that he "will help you." It is in knowing that God will strengthen you and help you that you can truly have hope.

Even beyond that, you do not need to face your recovery or even any struggle of life alone, for this passage assures you that "I am with you." You are not alone as God is with you and he will indeed help you. The quote from *Alcoholics Anonymous* indicates that your hopelessness of addiction is gradually replaced with a spiritual transformation of abundant hope and a sincere faith. Embrace this truth for yourself and be open to the hope, and strength, and help that God offers. With God in your life, you can truly have hope; God will help you be successful in recovery and with any struggle of life.

Additional Bible Passages
Key #2 - There Is Always Hope with God

Psalm 39:7 (NLT)
And so, Lord, where do I put my hope? My only hope is in you.

Psalm 31:24
Be strong and take heart, all you who hope in the Lord.

Isaiah 40:31
But those who hope in the Lord will renew their strength. They will soar on wings like eagles; they will run and not grow weary, they will walk and not be faint.

Joshua 1:9
Have I not commanded you? Be strong and courageous. Do not be afraid; do not be discouraged, for the Lord your God will be with you wherever you go."

Romans 15:13
May the God of hope fill you with all joy and peace as you trust in him, so that you may overflow with hope by the power of the Holy Spirit.

Closing Thoughts
Key #2 - There Is Always Hope with God

1) Because there is a God in heaven who has promised to help you, there is always hope with God.

2) Regardless of your past and even regardless of your current circumstance, you can trust God and he will help you.

3) Embrace the biblical message that God is with you and he will strengthen you and he will help you. With God in your life, there is always hope.

4) *Narcotics Anonymous* speaks about this hope and that it starts with God helping us and continues as we help others:
"We cannot deny other addicts their pain, but we can carry the message of hope that was given to us by fellow addicts in recovery. We share the principles of recovery, as they have worked in our lives. God helps us as we help each other. Life takes on a new meaning, a new joy, and a quality of being and feeling worthwhile. We become spiritually refreshed and are glad to be alive. One aspect of our spiritual awakening comes through the new understanding of our Higher Power that we develop by sharing another addict's recovery."[7]

Do You Want to Get Well?

**When Jesus saw him lying there and
learned that he had been in this condition
for a long time, he asked him,
"Do you want to get well?"
(John 5:6 NIV)**

===

"Do you want to get well and
are you willing to do whatever is necessary
to be successful in recovery?"[8]
(The Hope Recovery Devotional)

===

"I have been granted the gift of choice. I am no
longer at the mercy of a disease that tells me the
only answer is to drink. If willingness is the key
to unlock the gates of hell, it is action that opens
those doors so that we may walk freely among
the living.[9]
(Alcoholics Anonymous)

===

This passage of John 5:6 is a short verse, but yet it says so much. Jesus does not miss seeing the disabled man in bondage to his disease of many years and yet Jesus asks him a great question "Do you want to get well?" That might seem like a silly question, but it was a most appropriate question. There may have been many reasons that the man really did not want to get well. Later in the story, the man gives excuses why he could not be healed. However, Jesus intervenes and heals the man by telling him to "Pick up your mat and walk." (5:8) Jesus had compassion on the man and healed him to meet his physical needs and to reveal the power of God to change lives.

Perhaps you have been in bondage to your addiction for many years. God sees your bondage and your need and he wants to intervene in your life as well. But, first, how do you answer this question "Do you want to get well?" Do you want to get well and are you willing to do whatever is necessary to be successful in recovery? The quote from *Alcoholics Anonymous* also speaks to this same type of situation as it says, "I have been granted the gift of choice." You also have the gift of choice today. You can choose to do whatever is necessary to be successful in recovery. God wants to heal you so that the power of God in your life may impact not only you but many others as they see what God has done in your life. I encourage you to consider for yourself how you answer this question "Do you want to get well?" God wants to heal you. Be open to God's power in your life for a dramatically changed life.

Additional Bible Passages
Key #3 – Do You Want to Get Well?

Matthew 11:28
 Come to me, all you who are weary and burdened, and I will give you rest.

Matthew 14:13-14 (ESV)
But when the crowds heard it, they followed him on foot from the towns. [14] When he went ashore he saw a great crowd, and he had compassion on them and healed their sick.

Mark1:14 (NKJV)
Then Jesus, moved with compassion, stretched out *His* hand and touched him, and said to him, "I am willing; be cleansed."

Mark 9:23-24 (ESV)
 And Jesus said to him, "'If you can'! All things are possible for one who believes." [24] Immediately the father of the child cried out and said, "I believe; help my unbelief!"

Psalm 45:3-4
When I am afraid, I put my trust in you. [4]In God, whose word I praise—in God I trust and am not afraid.

Closing Thoughts
Key #3 – Do You Want to Get Well?

1) Are you truly ready to do whatever is necessary to be successful in recovery? That is when recovery starts.

2) Regardless of how many years you have been in your addiction, Jesus is asking you this question today "Do you want to get well?"

3) Commit today to do whatever is necessary to be successful in recovery and start by bringing God into your life.

4) Do not worry about all the details of your recovery for tomorrow, next week, or next month. God knows what you need. Trust God today to help you today and trust God to help you to live one day at a time.

5) *Alcoholics Anonymous* speaks about getting well and the importance of God in your life, stating:
"Burn the idea into the consciousness of every man that he can get well regardless of anyone. The only condition is that he trust in God and clean house.... If you persist, remarkable things will happen. When we look back, we realize that the things which came to us when we put ourselves in God's hands were better than anything we could have planned."[10]

Recovery Is Possible with God

**I can do all things through Christ
who strengthens me.
(Philippians 4:13 NKJV)**

===

"Don't let you past dictate your future. With
God recovery is absolutely possible."[11]
(The Hope Recovery Devotional)

===

"Our whole attitude and outlook upon
life will change....We will suddenly realize
that God is doing for us what we could not do
for ourselves."[12]
(Alcoholics Anonymous)

===

The books of *Alcoholics Anonymous* and *Narcotics Anonymous* speak about success in recovery through a spiritual experience with God. That is what the quote today from AA speaks of as well "that God is doing for us what we could not do for ourselves." The power of God is not dismissed or minimized, but it is embraced as critical for success in recovery. AA and NA encourage their readers to find their "Higher Power" and that through this "Higher Power" you can have success in recovery.

This quote from AA is also consistent with the passage from Philippians 4:13 "I can do all things through Christ who strengthens me." The instruction for you today is to rely on the strength that comes to you through faith in Jesus Christ. Lack of power was the problem, and it is the power of God that can give you the power to be successful in recovery. The power of God is indeed enough to help you be successful in recovery. The passage today speaks to this by stating, "I can do all things" through Christ who strengthens me. In addition, the AA quote speaks to this same point when it states, "Our whole attitude and outlook upon life will change." Life will not be perfect, but your perspective on life will be different! God will help you in ways that you could not do for yourself.

Your past life does not need to dictate your future life. Your future can be very different from your past. Recovery is absolutely possible with God in your life. Embrace the truth of Philippians 4:13 and be amazed at what God can do in your life.

Additional Bible Passages
Key #4 – Recovery Is Possible With God

John 10:10

The thief comes only to steal and kill and destroy; I have come that they may have life, and have it to the full.

Matthew 19:25-26

When the disciples heard this, they were greatly astonished and asked, "Who then can be saved?" [26] Jesus looked at them and said, "With man this is impossible, but with God all things are possible."

Psalm 147:5

Great is our Lord and mighty in power; his understanding has no limit.

Mark 5:36

As soon as Jesus heard the word that was spoken, He said to the ruler of the synagogue, "Do not be afraid; only believe."

John 11:40

Then Jesus said, "Did I not tell you that if you believe, you will see the glory of God?"

Closing Thoughts
Key #4 – Recovery Is Possible With God

1) Do not limit God in your life. With God in your life, recovery is absolutely possible.

2) Millions of people have been successful in recovery because of what God has done in their life through the Twelve Steps of Recovery.

3) Your past may be a terrible past, but I encourage you to leave your past in the past and embrace the truth that your future can be dramatically different from your past.

4) As you put your faith and trust in God through the Lord Jesus Christ, you will begin to see that you can do all things through Christ who gives you strength and this includes being successful in recovery.

5) *Narcotics Anonymous* speaks of trusting God and the dramatic change this can bring when it states: "We learned to trust God for help daily. Living just for today relieves the burden of the past and the fear of the future. We learned to take whatever actions are necessary and to leave the results in the hands of our Higher Power.... We receive guidance when we ask for knowledge of God's will for us. Gradually, as we become more God-centered than self-centered, our despair turns to hope.... Any clean addict is a miracle."[13]

God Wants to Forgive You

**He does not deal with us according to our sins....[11] For as high as the heavens are above the earth, so great is his steadfast love toward those who fear him; [12] as far as the east is from the west, so far does he remove our transgressions from us.
(Psalm 103:10-12 ESV)**

━━━━━━━━━━━━━━━━━━━━━━━━━━━━━━━━━━━━━━

"Regardless of what you have done in the past, God wants to forgive you!"[14]
(The Hope Recovery Devotional)

━━━━━━━━━━━━━━━━━━━━━━━━━━━━━━━━━━━━━━

"After making our review we ask God's forgiveness and inquire what corrective measures should be taken."[15]
(Alcoholics Anonymous)

━━━━━━━━━━━━━━━━━━━━━━━━━━━━━━━━━━━━━━

Forgiveness is often a very difficult topic for individuals in recovery. Perhaps it is difficult for you to accept God's forgiveness, or perhaps it is difficult for you to forgive yourself for all the hurt and pain you caused others. The verses today from Psalm 103 speak quite clearly of God's forgiveness. You may feel that you have committed many horrible sins in your past life that you doubt God could ever forgive you. You may even feel you are not sure you can forgive yourself. These very feelings are why I love these verses so much! This passage describes the forgiving heart of God to a repentant person. I suggest you read these verses again and perhaps even the entire chapter of 103, as it has much to say regarding forgiveness.

The first point to highlight is that God "does not deal with us according to our sins." This alone is a biblical truth to be so grateful for. Even beyond that, the passage states that God will remove them "as far as the east is from the west." It does not minimize the dreadful condition of our sin, but it states that God in his mercy will not deal with us "according to our sins." I encourage you to take the message of this passage to heart for your own situation and consider that "Regardless of what you have done in the past, God wants to forgive you!" God does not give up on you or any of us. It is with this type of godly forgiveness that the power of God can begin to work in your life. Accept God's forgiveness and begin to forgive yourself as well. God wants to forgive you. Why don't you let him?

Additional Bible Passages
Key #5 – God Wants to Forgive You

John 8:10-11 (ESV)
Jesus stood up and said to her, "Woman, where are they? Has no one condemned you?" [11] She said, "No one, Lord." And Jesus said, "Neither do I condemn you; go, and from now on sin no more."

1 John 2:1-2
My dear children, I write this to you so that you will not sin. But if anybody does sin, we have an advocate with the Father—Jesus Christ, the Righteous One. [2] He is the atoning sacrifice for our sins, and not only for ours but also for the sins of the whole world.

Luke 7:47-50 (ESV)
Therefore I tell you, her sins, which are many, are forgiven—for she loved much. But he who is forgiven little, loves little." [48] And he said to her, "Your sins are forgiven." [49] Then those who were at table with him began to say among themselves, "Who is this, who even forgives sins?" [50] And he said to the woman, "Your faith has saved you; go in peace."

Mark 2:5
When Jesus saw their faith, he said to the paralyzed man, "Son, your sins are forgiven."

Closing Thoughts
Key #5 – God Wants to Forgive You

1) You may feel you have committed many terrible sins in your addiction past, but please know that God does indeed want to forgive you.

2) Remember that God is a loving, caring, and compassionate God and that regardless of your past, God does not give up on you and he wants to forgive you.

3) God will not only forgive you of your sins, but he will remove them as far as the east is from the west. He simply wants you to turn back to him.

4) Accepting God's forgiveness can dramatically change your life. It will help you forgive yourself and to grow in your recovery and faith as well. *Alcoholics Anonymous* speaks about forgiveness with:
"If we are sorry for what we have done, and have the honest desire to let God take us to better things, we believe we will be forgiven and will have learned our lesson. If we are not sorry, and our conduct continues to harm others, we are quite sure to drink. We are not theorizing. These are facts out of our experience.... In this book you read again and again that faith did for us what we could not do for ourselves. We hope you are convinced now that God can remove whatever self-will has blocked you off from Him."[16]

Seek God and You Will Find Him

**You will seek me and find me
when you seek me with all of your heart.
(Jeremiah 29:13 NIV)**

===

"Seek God with all of your heart
and you will find him."[17]
(The Hope Recovery Devotional)

===

"For faith in a Power greater than ourselves, and miraculous demonstrations of that power in human lives, are facts as old as man himself. We finally saw that faith in some kind of God was a part of our make-up....Sometimes we had to search fearlessly, but He was there. He was as much a fact as we were."[18]
(Alcoholics Anonymous)

===

The books of *Alcoholics Anonymous, Narcotics Anonymous,* and the Bible all have much to say about seeking and finding God. These three books all speak quite strongly that if you seek God, you will indeed find him. The quote today from *Alcoholics Anonymous* puts it directly when it states, "We finally saw that faith in some kind of God was a part of our make-up....Sometimes we had to search fearlessly, but He was there." Amazingly, this AA quote is quite similar to the passage today from Jeremiah 29:13 "You will seek me and find me when you seek me with all of your heart."

The message of these books is clear that if you honestly seek to find God, you will indeed find him. Consider the magnitude of this statement! There is a God in heaven that is able and desiring to be found by you! Even beyond that, he is a loving, caring, compassionate, and powerful God who wants to help you! As AA says, there have been "miraculous demonstrations of that power" for all time. This is the type of "Higher Power" that AA and NA speak about, and it is the type of power that can help you be successful in recovery and even over any struggle of life.

Once you find God a transformation will begin to happen. You will seek to honor God before yourself. You will seek God's will in your life before your own. Your focus and your priority will now be on God and his will in your life. I encourage you to seek God with all of your heart, because if you do you will indeed find him.

Additional Bible Passages
Key #6 – Seek God and You Will Find Him

Isaiah 55:6-7
Seek the Lord while he may be found; call on him while he is near. [7] Let the wicked forsake their ways and the unrighteous their thoughts. Let them turn to the Lord, and he will have mercy on them, and to our God, for he will freely pardon.

Matthew 6:33
But seek first his kingdom and his righteousness, and all these things will be given to you as well.

Romans 10:13 (ESV)
For "everyone who calls on the name of the Lord will be saved."

2 Corinthians 6:1-2
As God's co-workers we urge you not to receive God's grace in vain. [2] For he says,"In the time of my favor I heard you, and in the day of salvation I helped you." I tell you, now is the time of God's favor, now is the day of salvation.

Hebrews 11:6 (ESV)
And without faith it is impossible to please him, for whoever would draw near to God must believe that he exists and that he rewards those who seek him.

Closing Thoughts
Key #6 – Seek God and You Will Find Him

1) AA and NA are both spiritual books and they both encourage you to seek to find God. Their approach is a great, welcoming way to bring God into the recovery process.

2) As you seek with all of your heart to find God, you will be led to the loving God of the Bible.

3) There are many ways to seek to find God, but the most important is to genuinely seek God with all of your heart. Certainly, also read the Bible, pray, read other spiritual books, and consider the evidence of the created world.

4) Seeking God is all about having a spiritual experience with God. Seek God and turn your life and your will over to him and your life will be transformed. *Alcoholics Anonymous* reflects this stating:
"The central fact of our lives today is the absolute certainty that our Creator has entered into our hearts and lives in a way which is indeed miraculous. He has commenced to accomplish those things for us which we could never do by ourselves."[19]

Jesus Is the True Higher Power

**Jesus answered, "I am the way, and the truth, and the life. No one comes to the Father except through me."
(John 14:5-6 NIV)**

===

"Jesus is the way, the truth, and the life and
Jesus is the true Higher Power."
(The Hope Recovery Devotional)

===

"My friend suggested what then seemed a novel idea. He said, 'Why don't you choose your own conception of God?' That statement hit me hard. It melted the icy intellectual mountain in whose shadow I had lived and shivered many years. I stood in the sunlight at last. It was only a matter of being willing to believe in a Power greater than myself. Nothing more was required of me to make my beginning."[20]
(Alcoholics Anonymous)

===

The Bible does not use the specific words of "Higher Power", but really "Higher Power" is simply another way to refer to God. AA and NA use the phrase "Higher Power" as a general way to refer to God. It is commonly understood that "Higher Power" certainly refers to God.

In the passage today from John 14:5-6 Jesus makes a great declaration about himself stating "I am the way, and the truth, and the life. No one comes to the Father except through me." Many understand this as Jesus declaring that he is the Christ, the Son of God. Using the terminology of AA and NA Jesus is declaring that he is the true "Higher Power." It is declarations like this one and many more throughout the Bible that all point to Jesus as the Son of God who came to earth to provide a way of salvation and redemption for all of humanity and specifically for you as well. Jesus came to earth to be a servant to mankind, to help us in our bondage to sin, and to show us that there is indeed a better way. In essence Jesus came to earth to help us, to help people, to be a servant, and to restore our relationship with God. It is another amazing similarity of AA, NA, and the Bible that they all have such a focus on service, on helping others, and on restoring our relationship with the true "Higher Power".

I encourage you to read the Bible, perhaps start with the Gospel of John, and as you read it consider the descriptions of Jesus as just other ways to refer to him as the true "Higher Power."

Additional Bible Passages
Key #7 – Jesus Is the True Higher Power

John 20:30-31 (ESV)

Now Jesus did many other signs in the presence of the disciples, which are not written in this book; [31] but these are written so that you may believe that Jesus is the Christ, the Son of God, and that by believing you may have life in his name.

John 1:14

The Word became flesh and made his dwelling among us. We have seen his glory, the glory of the one and only Son, who came from the Father, full of grace and truth.

John 20:27-29 (ESV)

Then he said to Thomas, "Put your finger here; see my hands. Reach out your hand and put it into my side. Stop doubting and believe." [28] Thomas said to him, "My Lord and my God!" [29] Then Jesus told him, "Because you have seen me, you have believed; blessed are those who have not seen and yet have believed."

Matthew 16:15-17 (ESV)

He said to them, "But who do you say that I am?" [16] Simon Peter replied, "You are the Christ, the Son of the living God." [17] And Jesus answered him, "Blessed are you, Simon Bar-Jonah! For flesh and blood has not revealed this to you, but my Father who is in heaven.

Closing Thoughts
Key #7 – Jesus Is the True Higher Power

1) Do not focus on religion, or any church, or even any pastor, but focus on God. Focus on having a spiritual experience with God.

2) AA and NA both speak about a "Higher Power". I encourage you to consider that the true "Higher Power" is revealed in the Bible as the Lord Jesus Christ.

3) In many ways Jesus declares that about himself when he states "I am the way, and the truth, and the life. No one comes to the Father except through me."

4) The phrase "Higher Power" is simply another way to refer to God. Seek God and let the "Higher Power" of the Bible transform your life. *Alcoholics Anonymous* speaks to this point with:
"Lack of power, that was our dilemma. We had to find a power by which we could live, and it had to be a *Power greater than ourselves.* Obviously. But where and how were we to find this Power? Well, that's exactly what this book is about. Its main object is to enable you to find a Power greater than yourself which will solve your problem. That means we have written a book which we believe to be spiritual as well as moral. And it means, of course, that we are going to talk about God."[21]

Make a Decision to Put Your Faith in Jesus

For God so loved the world that he gave his one and only Son, that whoever believes in him shall not perish but have eternal life. (John 3:16 NIV)

===

"Put your faith and trust in Jesus
as the true Higher Power."[22]
(The Hope Recovery Devotional)

===

"Surrendering our will puts us in contact with a Higher Power who fills the empty place inside that nothing could ever fill. We learned to trust God for help daily. Living just for today relieves the burden of the past and the fear of the future."[23]
(Narcotics Anonymous)

===

The verse today of John 3:16 is perhaps the best known passage of the Bible. It is a verse that beautifully captures the message of the entire Bible in one amazing verse. This one verse is full of many important details. It describes why God did what he did by stating, "For God so loved the world." God sent Jesus into the world because he "so loved the world." What a great declaration about God and about Jesus as well. The verse describes that God gave "his one and only Son" to die on the cross for the sins of the world. It is through this act of redemption on the cross that the world might have a right relationship with God, restored through faith in the Lord Jesus Christ. It is through this decision of faith in Jesus that you can have ultimate freedom from sin and eternal life as well. *Narcotics Anonymous* speaks of "Surrendering our will puts us in contact with a Higher Power who fills the empty place inside that nothing could ever fill." Respond to God's love for the world to fill the God-sized hole that nothing else could fill.

Another way to read this verse is "For God so loved you", because that really is what the verse is all about. As with Step Three of Recovery, this key #8 says to "Make a decision to put your faith in Jesus." It means for you to make a decision, to make a choice to put your faith and trust in Jesus. You do not earn your grace or your redemption, but it is a free gift of God by grace through faith in the Lord Jesus Christ. I encourage you to accept the message of this great verse and begin a brand new life in Christ.

Additional Bible Passages
Key #8 – Make a Decision to Put
Your Faith in Jesus

Acts 16:30-31 (ESV)

Then he brought them out and said, "Sirs, what must I do to be saved?" [31] And they said, "Believe in the Lord Jesus, and you will be saved, you and your household."

Ephesians 2:8-9

For it is by grace you have been saved, through faith— and this is not from yourselves, it is the gift of God— [9] not by works, so that no one can boast.

Romans 6:23 (ESV)

For the wages of sin is death, but the free gift of God is eternal life in Christ Jesus our Lord.

Acts 4:11-12 (ESV)

This Jesus is the stone that was rejected by you, the builders, which has become the cornerstone. [12] And there is salvation in no one else, for there is no other name under heaven given among men by which we must be saved."

John 3:3 (ESV)

Jesus answered him, "Truly, truly, I say to you, unless one is born again he cannot see the kingdom of God."

**Closing Thoughts
Key #8 – Make a Decision to Put
Your Faith in Jesus**

1) The main message of the Bible is expressed in John 3:16 and it begins with "For God so loved the world that he gave his one and only Son...." God loves the world and he loves you as well.

2) A right standing with God is not about rules and regulations, but it is about a restored relationship with God by grace through faith in the Lord Jesus Christ.

3) Leave your past negative experiences of faith, church, and God in the past and consider having a brand new spiritual experience with the true "Higher Power" of the Bible, the Lord Jesus Christ.

4) *Alcoholics Anonymous* speaks about fully turning your life over to God when it states:
"So after reviewing these things and realizing what liquor had cost me, I went to this Higher Power that, to me, was God, without any reservation, and admitted that I was completely powerless over alcohol and that I was willing to do anything in the world to get rid of the problem. In fact, I admitted that from then on I was willing to let God take over instead of me."[24]

Surround Yourself with Like-Minded People

**Do not be misled:
"Bad company corrupts good character."
(1 Corinthians 15:33 NIV)**

===

"Surround yourself with like-minded people that share your desire to be clean and sober and share your love for God."[25]
(The Hope Recovery Devotional)

===

"Now clean and in the Fellowship, we need to keep ourselves surrounded by others who know us well. We need each other."[26]
(Narcotics Anonymous)

===

The passage today from 1 Corinthians 15:33 is another great demonstration that God knows us inside and out. This verse was true 2000 years ago and is still true today. Certainly, it is critical for you in recovery, but it is also an important biblical truth for all believers as well. For you in recovery, this simple verse is quite powerful even with the opening caution of "Do not be misled." You may feel you are ok to keep your old friends and still go to your old familiar hangouts, but this verse states the wise words of warning "Do not be misled."

The second portion of the verse "Bad company corrupts good character" is also quite insightful. The people that you spend time with are the people that will influence you. The people, places, and things that you are around will indeed influence you. It may be gradual, but it will definitely happen. What type of person do you want to influence you? What type of person do you want to become? The admonition of this lesson is simply to "surround yourself with like-minded people that share your desire to be clean and sober and that share your love for God!" This will likely mean you need to leave many past friends in the past and begin new friendships with people that share your desire to be clean and sober and share your love for God. Nurture new connections and friendships that will indeed support your new life in recovery and with God. Cling to the *Narcotics Anonymous* message that "We need each other." Embrace the message of this verse to surround yourself with like-minded people.

Additional Bible Passages
Key #9 – Surround Yourself with Like-Minded People

Hebrews 10:24-25
And let us consider how we may spur one another on toward love and good deeds, [25] not giving up meeting together, as some are in the habit of doing, but encouraging one another—and all the more as you see the Day approaching.

1 Thessalonians 5:11
Therefore encourage one another and build each other up, just as in fact you are doing.

Ephesians 4:31-32 (ESV)
Let all bitterness and wrath and anger and clamor and slander be put away from you, along with all malice. [32] Be kind to one another, tenderhearted, forgiving one another, as God in Christ forgave you.

Mark 10:45
For even the Son of Man did not come to be served, but to serve, and to give his life as a ransom for many."

Proverbs 27:17 (ESV)
Iron sharpens iron, and one man sharpens another.

Closing Thoughts
Key #9 – Surround Yourself with Like-Minded People

1) It is important to be intentional with your friends in recovery. You will need to remove old friends and add new friends, all guided by the principle of surrounding yourself with like-minded people that share your desire to be clean and sober and share your love for God.

2) The Bible quote today is still true today that bad company does indeed corrupt good character. Do not be misled, but be wise and thoughtful as you make wise and hard decisions regarding your friends.

3) Leave your old people, places, and things in the past and embrace new people, places, and things that support your recovery and support your relationship with God.

4) *Narcotics Anonymous* reflects the importance of surrounding yourself with new friends that share your desire to be clean and sober when it says:
"The ultimate weapon for recovery is the recovering addict. We concentrate on recovery and feelings not what we have done in the past. Old friends, places and ideas are often a threat to our recovery. We need to change our playmates, playgrounds and playthings."[27]

God Made You for a Purpose

**"For I know the plans I have for you,"
declares the Lord, "plans to prosper you
and not to harm you, plans to give you
hope and a future."
(Jeremiah 29:11 NIV)**

==

"God has made you for a purpose; consider
what has God called you to do?"[28]
(The Hope Recovery Devotional)

==

"As we grow spiritually we become attuned to
our feelings and our purpose in life. By loving
ourselves, we become able to truly love others.
This is a spiritual awakening that comes as a
result of living this program. We find ourselves
daring to care and love!"[29]
(Narcotics Anonymous)

==

The passage today speaks about God having a plan and purpose for the prophet Jeremiah, and in the same way, God has a plan and a purpose for you. When was the last time you considered you were made by God with a purpose and a plan for your life? God has given you many unique skills and abilities, and God has indeed made you for a purpose. While it is important to work at a job for income to pay the bills, God has created you for much more than that. God has created you "to give you hope and a future."

Just as Jesus came to earth not to be served, but to serve, you are here on earth to be of service to others as well. Regardless of what job or occupation you have, ultimately you are here to honor God and to serve people in some way. God has made you for a purpose; consider what has God called you to do? God can use even your years in addiction as valuable life experience where you can help others to also be successful in recovery, as only someone who has been in addiction can do.

As you consider God made you for a purpose you might see that God is changing the direction of your life in a very unexpected way. Be open to how God might direct your life to something new, perhaps going back to school, to college, or a brand new career direction. *Narcotics Anonymous* speaks to this saying, "As we grow spiritually we become attuned to our feelings and our purpose in life." Be mindful that God has "plans to give you hope and a future" and then be amazed at how God directs your life with a brand new future.

Additional Bible Passages
Key #10 – God Made You for a Purpose

Jeremiah 1:4-5

The word of the Lord came to me, saying,[5] "Before I formed you in the womb I knew you, before you were born I set you apart; I appointed you as a prophet to the nations."

Psalm 139:13-14

For you created my inmost being; you knit me together in my mother's womb. [14] I praise you because I am fearfully and wonderfully made; your works are wonderful, I know that full well.

Matthew 4:18-20 (ESV)

While walking by the Sea of Galilee, he saw two brothers, Simon (who is called Peter) and Andrew his brother, casting a net into the sea, for they were fishermen. [19] And he said to them, "Follow me, and I will make you fishers of men." [20] Immediately they left their nets and followed him.

Proverbs 19:21 (ESV)

Many are the plans in a person's heart, but it is the Lord's purpose that prevails.

Closing Thoughts
Key #10 – God Made You for a Purpose

1) You are fearfully and wonderfully made and God has made you for a purpose. While you may not feel that way right now, that is the truth of Scripture.

2) God has gifted you in many unique ways for a particular purpose. God can use even the terrible events of your past life and combine them with your gifts and abilities to honor God and to help people as well.

3) Jesus called the apostles to leave their role as fisherman and he called them to a new role as "fishers of men". Their calling and purpose was then very different from what they might have expected.

4) Consider today what God might be calling you to and what your purpose might be with God in your life.

5) *Alcoholics Anonymous* talks about purpose in life beyond ourselves when it states:
"Those of us who have spent much time in the world of spiritual make-believe have eventually seen the childishness of it. This dream world has been replaced by a great sense of purpose, accompanied by a growing consciousness of the power of God in our lives.... We have found nothing incompatible between a powerful spiritual experience and a life of sane and happy usefulness."

Peace That Surpasses All Understanding

**And the peace of God, which surpasses all understanding, will guard your hearts and your minds in Christ Jesus.
(Philippians 4:7 ESV)**

===

"You will still have struggles, but with God in your life you can have 'a peace that surpasses all understanding'."
(The Hope Recovery Devotional)

===

"So, as I have worked the program,
I have grown emotionally and intellectually.
I not only have peace with God, I have
the peace of God through an active God
consciousness. I have not only recovered from
alcoholism, I have become whole in person—
body, spirit, soul."[30]
(Alcoholics Anonymous)

===

As you grow in your recovery and in your faith, you will also grow in the peace of God in your life. The peace of God in your life is an amazing blessing and one that can only come through a relationship with God through the Lord Jesus Christ. This passage today from Philippians 4:7 is a great verse and wonderfully describes this peace of God, saying it is a peace which "surpasses all understanding." This peace of God is a peace that is not possible any other way. Perhaps you sought peace or fulfilment through drugs, sex, or money, and were always left lacking. Ultimately, true peace comes by knowing God is in control and that you can indeed trust God with your very life. To have the peace of God in your life will enable you to lay your head down at night and have peace and calmness in your mind, body, and spirit. *Alcoholics Anonymous* speaks to this and says, "I have become whole in person—body, spirit, soul."

Having the peace of God in your life does not mean that life will be perfect. You will still have struggles of life and things will still go wrong, but with God in your life, you can trust him to give you wisdom, guidance, and strength through any struggle or challenge of life. Having this peace of God in your life will "guard your hearts and your minds in Christ Jesus." The peace of God will help protect you and keep your mind focused on God so that you can continue to be successful in recovery. You then have the wonderful opportunity to share with others this tremendous peace that surpasses all understanding!

Additional Bible Passages
Key #11 – Peace That Surpasses
All Understanding

Romans 5:1 (ESV)
Therefore, since we have been justified by faith, we have peace with God through our Lord Jesus Christ.

Colossians 3:15-16
Let the peace of Christ rule in your hearts, since as members of one body you were called to peace. And be thankful.

John 16:33
"I have told you these things, so that in me you may have peace. In this world you will have trouble. But take heart! I have overcome the world."

Philippians 4:11-13 (ESV)
Not that I am speaking of being in need, for I have learned in whatever situation I am to be content. [12] I know how to be brought low, and I know how to abound. In any and every circumstance, I have learned the secret of facing plenty and hunger, abundance and need. [13] I can do all things through him who strengthens me.

Closing Thoughts
Key #11 – Peace That Surpasses All Understanding

1) We all have a "God sized hole". The deception is that all we need is just a little bit more and then we will be happy and then we will have peace. However, we are always left terribly lacking.

2) How have you been trying to fill this hole for yourself? Ture happiness and peace in life can only come from a restored relationship with God.

3) As you bring God into your life, you can indeed have peace, even a peace that surpasses all understanding. Life will not be perfect and you will still have difficulties and challenges, but God will help you through any struggle. This peace of God will enable you to lay your head down at night and have peace and calmness in your mind, body, and spirit.

4) *Narcotics Anonymous* speaks of this peace as: "We find ourselves praying, because it brings us peace and restores our confidence and courage. It helps us to live a life that is free of fear and distrust. When we remove our selfish motives and pray for guidance, we find feelings of peace and serenity.... As we seek our personal contact with God, we begin to open up as a flower in the sun. We begin to see that God's love has been present all the time, just waiting for us to accept it."[31]

Continue to Trust God
No Matter What

**Trust in the Lord with all your heart;
do not depend on your own
understanding.[6] Seek his will in all you do,
and he will show you which path to take.
(Proverbs 3:5-6 NLT)**

===

"No matter what happens continue to put your
faith and trust in God and he will give you
guidance and wisdom."[32]
(The Hope Recovery Devotional)

===

"We learned to trust God for help daily. Living
just for today relieves the burden of the past and
the fear of the future. We learned to take
whatever actions are necessary and to leave the
results in the hands of our Higher Power."[33]
(Narcotics Anonymous)

===

The passage today from Proverbs 3:5-6 shares a great message for growing in your recovery and for growing in your faith. The main instruction for today is to simply remember to "Continue to trust God no matter what." Life will be full of many ups and downs, but regardless of what happens, I encourage you to continue to trust God no matter what! The beginning of this passage states, "Trust in the Lord with all your heart; do not depend on your own understanding." What great wisdom and guidance! Do not depend on your own understanding, but trust in the Lord with all your heart. This instruction is valid and wise because you can trust God to help you. It may not be the path you would like, but you can trust God to guide you in the best way for you.

In addition, the second portion of this passage says to "Seek his will in all you do, and he will show you which path to take." As you seek to be obedient to God's will in your life, he will indeed direct your paths. You are to seek his will in all things, not just some, but all things. *Narcotics Anonymous* speaks to this stating, "We learned to trust God for help daily." Trusting God is not a once in a while thing! It is an everyday thing and even many times throughout the day. Even further, *Narcotics Anonymous* indicates to take whatever actions are necessary and then "to leave the results in the hands of our Higher Power." You can leave the results with God because you can trust God. I encourage you to embrace this truth to "Seek his will in all you do, and he will show you which path to take."

Additional Bible Passages
Key #12 – Continue to Trust God
No Matter What

Psalm 28:7

The Lord is my strength and my shield; in him my heart trusts, and I am helped; my heart exults, and with my song I give thanks to him.

Isaiah 41:10

So do not fear, for I am with you; do not be dismayed, for I am your God. I will strengthen you and help you; I will uphold you with my righteous right hand.

John 14:1

Do not let your hearts be troubled. You believe in God; believe also in me.

Isaiah 26:3-4

You will keep in perfect peace those whose minds are steadfast, because they trust in you. [4] Trust in the Lord forever, for the Lord, the Lord himself, is the Rock eternal.

Closing Thoughts
Key #12 – Continue to Trust God
No Matter What

1) Regardless of what might happen in life, you are to continue to trust God. You will still have difficulties in life. Bad things will still happen, but regardless, you are to continue to trust God with all of your heart.

2) Part of this trusting is to not lean on your own understanding. You are to trust God and his will in your life and not what you think might be best.

3) I encourage you to continue with the commitment to do whatever is necessary to be successful in recovery. As you continue to trust God, you will grow in your recovery and in your faith.

4) With these twelve keys of faith-based recovery, you can indeed have a dramatically changed life.

5) *Alcoholics Anonymous* has much to say about trusting God as it states:
"Perhaps there is a better way—we think so. For we are now on a different basis; the basis of trusting and relying upon God. We trust infinite God rather than our finite selves. We are in the world to play the role He assigns. Just to the extent that we do as we think He would have us, and humbly rely on Him, does He enable us to match calamity with serenity."[34]

The Twelve Steps of Alcoholics Anonymous

1. We admitted we were powerless over alcohol—that our lives had become unmanageable.
2. Came to believe that a Power greater than ourselves could restore us to sanity.
3. Made a decision to turn our will and our lives over to the care of God *as we understood Him.*
4. Made a searching and fearless moral inventory of ourselves.
5. Admitted to God, to ourselves, and to another human being the exact nature of our wrongs.
6. Were entirely ready to have God remove all these defects of character.
7. Humbly asked Him to remove our shortcomings.
8. Made a list of all persons we had harmed, and became willing to make amends to them all.
9. Made direct amends to such people wherever possible, except when to do so would injure them or others.
10. Continued to take personal inventory and when we were wrong promptly admitted it.
11. Sought through prayer and meditation to improve our conscious contact with God *as we understood Him,* praying only for knowledge of His will for us and the power to carry that out.
12. Having had a spiritual awakening as the result of these steps, we tried to carry this message to alcoholics, and to practice these principles in all our affairs.

The Twelve Steps of Narcotics Anonymous

1. We admitted that we were powerless over our addiction, that our lives had become unmanageable.
2. We came to believe that a Power greater than ourselves could restore us to sanity.
3. We made a decision to turn our will and our lives over to the care of God as we understood Him.
4. We made a searching and fearless moral inventory of ourselves.
5. We admitted to God, to ourselves, and to another human being the exact nature of our wrongs.
6. We were entirely ready to have God remove all these defects of character.
7. We humbly asked Him to remove our shortcomings.
8. We made a list of all persons we had harmed, and became willing to make amends to them all.
9. We made direct amends to such people wherever possible, except when to do so would injure them or others.
10. We continued to take personal inventory and when we were wrong promptly admitted it.
11. We sought through prayer and meditation to improve our conscious contact with God as we understood Him, praying only for knowledge of His will for us and the power to carry that out.
12. Having had a spiritual awakening as a result of these steps, we tried to carry this message to addicts, and to practice these principles in all our affairs.

The Serenity Prayer (Short Version)

God grant me the serenity
To accept the things I cannot change;
Courage to change the things I can;
And wisdom to know the difference.
Amen.

The Serenity Prayer (Long Version)

God grant me the serenity
To accept the things I cannot change;
Courage to change the things I can;
And wisdom to know the difference.
Living one day at a time;
Enjoying one moment at a time;
Accepting hardships as the pathway to peace;
Taking, as He did, this sinful world
As it is, not as I would have it;
Trusting that He will make things right
If I surrender to His Will;
So that I may be reasonably happy in this life
And supremely happy with Him
Forever and ever in the next.
Amen

The Lord's Prayer

Our Father, who art in heaven,

hallowed be thy name;

thy kingdom come;

thy will be done;

on earth as it is in heaven.

Give us this day our daily bread.

And forgive us our trespasses,

as we forgive those who trespass against us.

And lead us not into temptation;

but deliver us from evil.

For thine is the kingdom,

the power and the glory,

for ever and ever.

Amen.

The Simple Addicts Prayer

Please God help me!

Prayer of Saint Francis

Lord, make me an instrument of your peace.

Where there is hatred let me sow love;

Where there is injury, pardon;

Where there is doubt, faith;

Where there is despair, hope;

Where there is darkness, light;

Where there is sadness, joy.

O Divine Master,

grant that I may not so much seek

To be consoled as to console;

To be understood as to understand;

To be loved as to love.

For it is in giving that we receive;

It is in pardoning that we are pardoned;

And it is in dying that we are born to eternal life.

Amen.

Thank you for supporting Hope Recovery. For additional faith-based recovery resources for individuals, churches, and recovery ministries please see the website:

www.HopeRecovery.us

Here you will find information on the 100-day recovery devotional and other resources.

The Hope Recovery Devotional
There Is Always Hope With God

Please email me any feedback to:

HopeRecoveryUs@gmail.com

Footnotes

---

[1] Greg Schmalhofer, The Hope Recovery Devotional: There is Always Hope with God, (Lancaster, Pa,Schmalhofer,2021), 6,8,10,12,16,24,46,48,62,64,68,120,206.

[2] Greg Schmalhofer, The Hope Recovery Devotional: There is Always Hope with God, (Lancaster, Pa,Schmalhofer,2021), 6.

[3] Bill W., Alcoholics Anonymous: The Story of How Many Thousands of Men and Women Have Recovered from Alcoholism, (New York City NY, Alcoholics Anonymous World Services, Inc., 2001), 386-387.

[4] Bill W., Alcoholics Anonymous: The Story of How Many Thousands of Men and Women Have Recovered from Alcoholism, (New York City NY, Alcoholics Anonymous World Services, Inc., 2001), 55.

[5] Greg Schmalhofer, The Hope Recovery Devotional: There is Always Hope with God, (Lancaster, Pa,Schmalhofer,2021), 6.

[6] Bill W., Alcoholics Anonymous: The Story of How Many Thousands of Men and Women Have Recovered from Alcoholism, (New York City NY, Alcoholics Anonymous World Services, Inc., 2001), 475.

[7] Narcotics Anonymous, 6th ed. (Van Nuys, CA, Narcotics Anonymous World Services, Inc., 2008), 52-53.

[8] Greg Schmalhofer, The Hope Recovery Devotional: There is Always Hope with God, (Lancaster, Pa,Schmalhofer,2021), 6.

[9] Bill W., Alcoholics Anonymous: The Story of How Many Thousands of Men and Women Have Recovered from Alcoholism, (New York City NY, Alcoholics Anonymous World Services, Inc., 2001), 317.

[10] Bill W., Alcoholics Anonymous: The Story of How Many Thousands of Men and Women Have Recovered from Alcoholism, (New York City NY, Alcoholics Anonymous World Services, Inc., 2001), 98,100.

[11] Greg Schmalhofer, The Hope Recovery Devotional: There is Always Hope with God, (Lancaster, Pa,Schmalhofer,2021), 6.

[12] Bill W., Alcoholics Anonymous: The Story of How Many Thousands of Men and Women Have Recovered from Alcoholism, (New York City NY, Alcoholics Anonymous World Services, Inc., 2001), 84.

[13] Narcotics Anonymous, 6th ed. (Van Nuys, CA, Narcotics Anonymous World Services, Inc., 2008), 94,95.

[14] Greg Schmalhofer, The Hope Recovery Devotional: There is Always Hope with God, (Lancaster, Pa,Schmalhofer,2021), 6.

[15] Bill W., Alcoholics Anonymous: The Story of How Many Thousands of Men and Women Have Recovered from Alcoholism, (New York City NY, Alcoholics Anonymous World Services, Inc., 2001), 86.

[16] Bill W., Alcoholics Anonymous: The Story of How Many Thousands of Men and Women Have Recovered from Alcoholism, (New York City NY, Alcoholics Anonymous World Services, Inc., 2001), 70-71.

[17] Greg Schmalhofer, The Hope Recovery Devotional: There is Always Hope with God, (Lancaster, Pa,Schmalhofer,2021), 6.

[18] Bill W., Alcoholics Anonymous: The Story of How Many Thousands of Men and Women Have Recovered from Alcoholism, (New York City NY, Alcoholics Anonymous World Services, Inc., 2001), 55.

[19] Bill W., Alcoholics Anonymous: The Story of How Many Thousands of Men and Women Have Recovered from Alcoholism, (New York City NY, Alcoholics Anonymous World Services, Inc., 2001), 25.

[20] Bill W., Alcoholics Anonymous: The Story of How Many Thousands of Men and Women Have Recovered from Alcoholism, (New York City NY, Alcoholics Anonymous World Services, Inc., 2001), 12.

[21] Bill W., Alcoholics Anonymous: The Story of How Many Thousands of Men and Women Have Recovered from Alcoholism, (New York City NY, Alcoholics Anonymous World Services, Inc., 2001), 45.

[22] Greg Schmalhofer, The Hope Recovery Devotional: There is Always Hope with God, (Lancaster, Pa,Schmalhofer,2021), 7.

[23] Narcotics Anonymous, 6th ed. (Van Nuys, CA, Narcotics Anonymous World Services, Inc., 2008), 94.

[24] Bill W., Alcoholics Anonymous: The Story of How Many Thousands of Men and Women Have Recovered from Alcoholism, (New York City NY, Alcoholics Anonymous World Services, Inc., 2001), 187.

[25] Greg Schmalhofer, The Hope Recovery Devotional: There is Always Hope with God, (Lancaster, Pa,Schmalhofer,2021), 7.

[26] Narcotics Anonymous, 6th ed. (Van Nuys, CA, Narcotics Anonymous World Services, Inc., 2008), 83.

[27] Narcotics Anonymous, 6th ed. (Van Nuys, CA, Narcotics Anonymous World Services, Inc., 2008), 15-16.

[28] Greg Schmalhofer, The Hope Recovery Devotional: There is Always Hope with God, (Lancaster, Pa,Schmalhofer,2021), 7.

[29] Narcotics Anonymous, 6th ed. (Van Nuys, CA, Narcotics Anonymous World Services, Inc., 2008), 106.

[30] Bill W., Alcoholics Anonymous: The Story of How Many Thousands of Men and Women Have Recovered from Alcoholism, (New York City NY, Alcoholics Anonymous World Services, Inc., 2001), 457.

[31] Narcotics Anonymous, 6th ed. (Van Nuys, CA, Narcotics Anonymous World Services, Inc., 2008), 47.

[32] Greg Schmalhofer, The Hope Recovery Devotional: There is Always Hope with God, (Lancaster, Pa,Schmalhofer,2021), 7.

[33] Narcotics Anonymous, 6th ed. (Van Nuys, CA, Narcotics Anonymous World Services, Inc., 2008), 94.

[34] Bill W., Alcoholics Anonymous: The Story of How Many Thousands of Men and Women Have Recovered from Alcoholism, (New York City NY, Alcoholics Anonymous World Services, Inc., 2001), 68.